Inventors at Work

by Francelia Sevin

PEARSON

Scott
Foresman

Editorial Offices: Glenview, Illinois • Parsippany, New Jersey • New York, New York
Sales Offices: Needham, Massachusetts • Duluth, Georgia • Glenview, Illinois
Coppell, Texas • Ontario, California • Mesa, Arizona

ISBN: 0-328-13650-6

6 7 8 9 10 V0G1 14 13 12 11 10 09 08

What do you think of when someone says the word *inventor*? Maybe you think of a woman dressed in a white coat, surrounded by test tubes and working late into the night. Perhaps you think of a gray-haired doctor making wacky machines. Whatever you think of, the truth is that inventors are just real people. They come from all walks of life, and from all over the world. They are of all ages. Some might even be younger than you!

Brandon Whale was eight years old when he received recognition for the PaceMate, which helps people who have pacemakers for their hearts, like Brandon's mother. When patients are at home, they send data about their heart through an electronic bracelet to the hospital. This bracelet was too big for his mother, so Brandon found a way to make it smaller and more conductive, so it could send information better.

Just like other inventors, Brandon Whale saw a need and figured out how to fill it. That is exactly what inventing is. Someone works out a problem by putting things together in a whole new way.

Inventing is not new. It is part of being human. In fact, humans have been using tools they invented for thousands of years. It is unlikely that people will ever stop inventing. From making the first wheel and using fire to creating fuel-cell cars and visiting space, there seems to be no end to human creativity.

Humans constantly improve upon old inventions to make new ones. The first wheel paved the way for modern cars.

Exactly how do inventors go about the process of inventing? Most often, the first thing an inventor does is set a goal. That's how Maria Telkes began one of her inventions in the 1970s. She set a goal to heat a house without using polluting fuels such as coal, oil, or gas. After a lot of hard work, Telkes met her goal. Her solar heating system **converts** sunlight into energy that can heat a house.

Today, people all over the world use the sun's energy to heat their homes. Telkes's work also inspired other inventors to start using the sun's energy. Now we can use solar energy not only to heat our homes, but also to power our appliances, computers, and other tools.

After setting a goal, an inventor then asks questions. He or she reads and tries to find out as much as possible about how other inventors met their goals. This step takes time, but it saves a lot of work.

If the inventor skips this step, he or she ends up making the same mistakes others have. It would be like taking a test without reading the chapter or doing your homework. You wouldn't do very well.

These homes use energy from the sun gathered by solar panels.

After researching and studying the subject thoroughly, the inventor writes down his or her idea and draws a plan. Most often the plan is based on work that others have done, but with a new twist. The inventor sees something in a new way and puts it in the plan.

When the inventor is happy with the plan, he or she builds a model and tests it. Building a model costs less than building the real thing. It makes it easy to find out if the idea will work without spending a lot of time on the actual invention. It also lets the inventor test one part of the idea at a time.

The Eight Steps of Inventing

Follow these steps to see how inventors try out their ideas lots of times before they get them right.

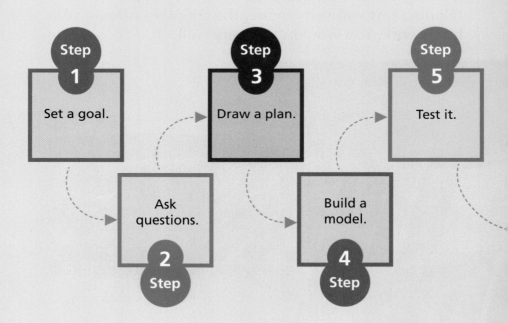

Step 1 — Set a goal.

Step 2 — Ask questions.

Step 3 — Draw a plan.

Step 4 — Build a model.

Step 5 — Test it.

A good inventor will work through eight steps of inventing, shown below. These steps are similar to what Wilbur and Orville Wright followed when they invented the first working airplane.

Long before Wilbur and Orville Wright flew their airplane for the first time in 1903, people had dreamed of taking to the sky. Many people in the past had tried to **devise** the perfect flying machine. Artist and inventor Leonardo da Vinci drew flying machines as far back as 1500. However, the dream of flying would have to wait for science to catch up.

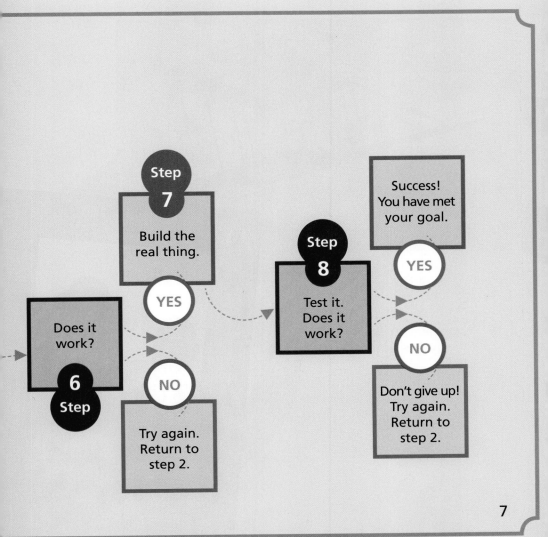

They set their goal at the start, which was to be the first to fly a powered machine that was heavier than air. Second, the Wrights asked questions. How do birds fly? What can we learn from them? What can we learn from inventions like the hot air balloon and the glider? The Wrights read as much as they could about flight and flying machines. By learning all they could, they made fewer mistakes.

The Wright brothers used what they had learned to draw a plan (step 3). Then the Wrights built a model (step 4). Sometimes the Wright brothers built kites to test their ideas. At other times, they built gliders.

Above is an example of one of the Wright brothers' gliders.

The Wright Brothers (center picture) finally got their airplane off the ground!

The Wrights tested their model one part at a time. That way, they knew which parts worked and which parts didn't. One by one, they tested wing shapes, propellers, engines, and many other parts. Only when they were sure that each piece of the machine worked on its own did they put them together. When the model worked, they built the real thing (step 7).

If you think following all these steps sounds like a lot of work, you're right. The Wright brothers spent years asking questions, building models, and testing them. If a model dove into the ground, they knew they had to rethink the airplane part they were testing. But every time one of their airplane parts worked, they knew they were getting closer.

All of their tests and questions paid off. They finally built an airplane that could fly. Imagine how the Wright brothers must have felt the first time they saw their machine leave the ground!

Before the late 1800s, big, heavy steam engines did most of the moving. Then gas engines were invented that were both strong and small. For the first time, something as heavy as an airplane could be lifted off of the ground. Suddenly lots of people started to draw plans for powered flying machines. Everyone wanted to be the first to fly.

European inventors had many different ideas about flying. Some inventors, such as Horatio Phillips, built flying machines that had a large number of wings. He called them multiplanes. Others tried to copy the way birds fly. Edward Purkis Frost believed ornithopters, aircraft with flapping wings, were the way to go. Still other inventors were inspired by wings. Percy Pilcher named his gliding machine the *Gull,* while Emilien Marceau called his the *Butterfly.*

Inventors also put more than one mechanism together in their flying machines. In 1902, Henri Villard from France built the *Aviator*. It combined features of both parachutes and helicopters.

These early attempts at flight were not always popular. One news reporter called M. Givaudan's 1909 "circular aeroplane" a "freakish machine."

Horatio Phillips's 1893 multiplane rose only a few feet off the ground. He built a different multiplane in 1907.

Edward Purkis Frost tried to copy the way a crow flies. He built ornithopters from 1902 to 1904.

Percy Pilcher's *Gull* was an early hang glider.

The flying machines people invented back then may seem funny to us now. But as Samuel Smiles (1812–1904) wrote:

> *We learn wisdom from failure much more than from success; we often discover what will do by finding out what will not do; and probably he who never made a mistake, never made a discovery.*

Akhil Madhani, the inventor of the surgical robot, feels much the same. He says, "In order to have good ideas, inventors have a lot of bad ideas too." Madhani won the Lemelson-MIT Student Prize in 1998 for one of his inventions. Most often, people work very hard for many years—and make many mistakes—before they are happy with their inventions.

Akhil Madhani, the inventor of the surgical robot. Photo by Barry Hetherington, courtesy of the Lemelson-MIT program.

The Mauve Mistake

Not all inventions happen by following the eight steps of inventing. Some happen by accident, but the inventors still recognize the value of their mistake.

In 1856 William Henry Perkin invented the first dye not made from plants. But Perkin was not trying to invent dye. He was trying to make a medicine from coal tars. Something went wrong, and Perkin ended up with a gooey black mess. When he tried to clean it up using rubbing alcohol, the black mess turned purple.

Perkin admired the color and thought that he could use it to dye silk. Perkin recognized the value of his mistake. He named the purple dye *mauve*. After Perkin's discovery, other artificial dyes were made. Because of the popularity of mauve and other dyes, the chemical industry flourished.

William Henry Perkin discovered his mauve dye by accident.

When inventors finally have an idea that works, they patent it. A patent is a law stating that no one else has the right to use the inventor's idea without paying the inventor. If someone can make money from selling the invention to people, the inventor must be paid a **percentage** of the profits.

Thomas Jefferson, who was an inventor himself, oversaw the Patent Act of 1790. People like to say that this law "invented inventing." After the law was passed, more people started to invent because they could own their ideas.

However, Jefferson did not believe in owning ideas. He never patented any of his own inventions. One of them, the cipher wheel, made secret ciphers, or codes, that no one else could break. But the cipher wheel did not catch on and people forgot about it. Many years later, when World War I began, the United States Army reinvented it and used it to send messages in code.

Thomas Jefferson (left) and a cipher wheel (above)

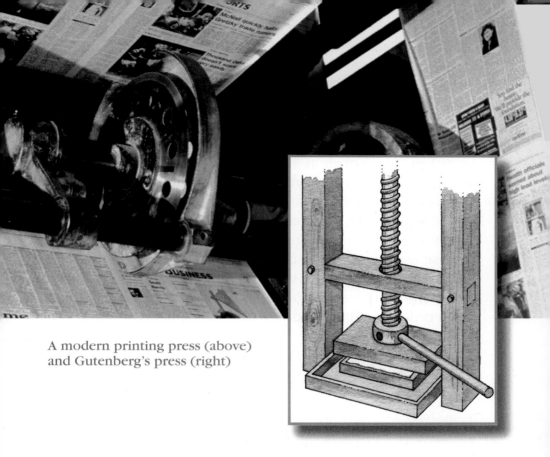

A modern printing press (above)
and Gutenberg's press (right)

The code wheel is just one of many inventions that have been reinvented. Printing with movable type was also invented twice. It was first invented in China by Bi Sheng in 1045. Four hundred years later, Johannes Gutenberg reinvented movable type in Germany in the form of the printing press. When he did, Europeans were able to **reproduce** books and newspapers faster than before. They no longer had to copy books by hand one at a time. Now they could make many more copies of the same book. More people could have books, so more people learned to read.

More than one person invented the telephone as well. We take the telephone for granted, but in 1876 people were amazed by this invention. For the first time, the sound of their voices could be **transmitted** across wires from one place to another.

The newspapers **proclaimed** Alexander Graham Bell as the inventor of the telephone in 1876. We still think of Bell as the inventor of the telephone because his version was the one that became widely used. In fact, Antonio Meucci invented the first true telephone around 1849. Later, both Elisha Gray and Alexander Graham Bell invented telephones in 1876. Bell filed for his patent just a few hours before Gray!

Since then, inventors have continued to make the telephone better. Fiber optic cables and voice mail are just two of the inventions that have made telephones a more useful means of communication. Today we use cellular phones with no wires at all to talk to each other.

Telephones are a good example of how inventors build on each other's work. Another is the light bulb. In the 1870s most homes were lit with candles, or gas or oil lamps. Their light was not very bright and the flames sometimes started fires.

Alexander Graham Bell (right)

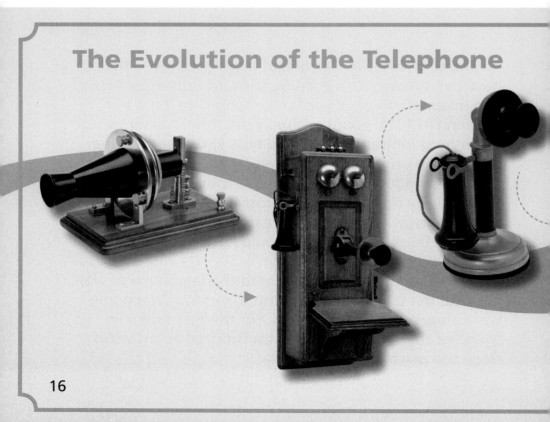

The Evolution of the Telephone

Thomas Edison also improved upon an earlier invention. Like many other inventors, he wanted to use electricity to make an artificial light that was bright and safe. Edison bought the light bulb patent from Henry Woodward and Matthew Evans and set to work making it better.

At the same time, in England, Joseph Wilson Swan was working on a light bulb that would stay lit for a long time. Swan was the first to invent a long-lasting bulb. It **generated** light for 13.5 hours without burning out.

In 1879 Thomas Edison made a light bulb too. Edison tried to make his light bulb more useful so that people would want to buy it. He tested six thousand filaments (wires that glow inside the bulb) to find one that would glow for a long time without burning out. Eventually Edison made a bulb that could last more than 1,200 hours.

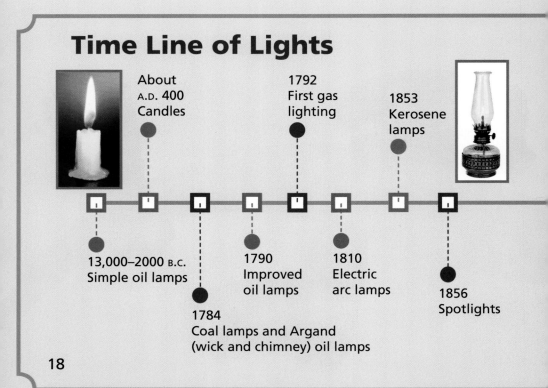

Time Line of Lights

About A.D. 400
Candles

1792
First gas lighting

1853
Kerosene lamps

13,000–2000 B.C.
Simple oil lamps

1790
Improved oil lamps

1810
Electric arc lamps

1856
Spotlights

1784
Coal lamps and Argand (wick and chimney) oil lamps

Edison also invented screw-in sockets for his light bulbs, light switches, and many other mechanisms that helped make electric lights easy to use. Soon it seemed as though everyone in the United States had electric lights.

But the story of electric light doesn't end there. By 1908 William David Coolidge had invented a new filament that improved the **efficiency** of light bulbs. They lasted longer than ever before, and cost less to use. Because his filament works so well, we still use it in light bulbs today.

Not only have people kept making the light bulb better, but they have also invented new kinds of lights. Some lights were invented to help indoor plants grow. Others were made to light large areas. Inventors have also made sun lamps, high-powered searchlights, black lights, neon lights, halogen lights, and laser lights. Look at the time line of lights to see just how far we've come.

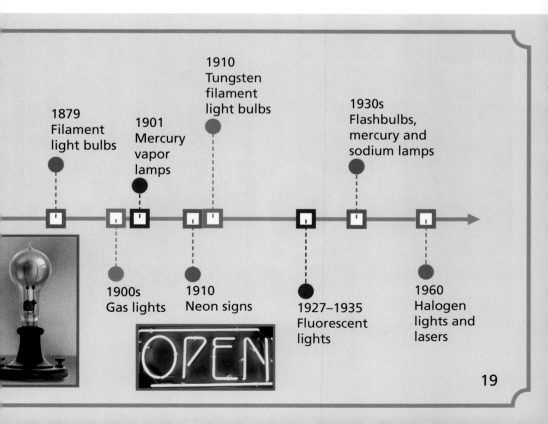

1879
Filament
light bulbs

1901
Mercury
vapor
lamps

1910
Tungsten
filament
light bulbs

1930s
Flashbulbs,
mercury and
sodium lamps

1900s
Gas lights

1910
Neon signs

1927–1935
Fluorescent
lights

1960
Halogen
lights and
lasers

Things are never quite the same after an invention comes into use. Inventions revolutionize our world. They change the way we live, work, think, and even dream. Can you picture what your life would be like if there were no cars? Not only would there be no cars, there would be no paved roads, no gas stations, and no traffic jams. There might be less air pollution, and distances might seem farther. Maybe there would be more trains. Perhaps you would ride a horse to school.

The automobile, like other modern inventions, has changed so many things that we can scarcely imagine life without it. They can change our lives in ways that we never thought of. Although we praise inventions for helping us do things better and faster, inventions have their disadvantages as well.

An early automobile

A modern traffic jam

Let's look at the changes the car has brought. Cars have lots of good points. They make it easy to go places whenever we want. And wherever we are going, we get there fast. They are comfortable, and many people enjoy driving.

Cars also have downsides. We must alter the landscape in order to build roads. Cars that use petroleum fuel create air pollution, which can cause illnesses. Car accidents are also a problem.

What if people at the turn of the century had known what the automobile would bring—the positives and the negatives? Would they still have chosen to use cars? We'll never know the answer to that question, but it can help us to think about inventions today. We need to ask questions about who benefits from inventions, and how they affect the environment, our health, and our lives. By looking at the good and the bad, we can choose when and how we want inventions to be used.

Now that you have read about some specific inventions, the process of inventing, patents, and the positives and negatives of inventions, you can start thinking about something you might invent. If you can keep an open mind, like Perkin did when he invented mauve, you may stumble across something you had not thought of before.

Inventiveness is a way of looking at the world, a way of living each day. Instead of seeing things in the same old way, try to see them with new eyes. Look around. Everything provides an opportunity to invent.

My Eight Steps of Inventing

Step 1

Set a goal.

Start by thinking about something in your life that bugs you—maybe something is too tall for you to use easily or a chore takes longer than you would like. Write down your goal as a sentence.

Step 2

Ask questions.

What can you do to fix it? What are all the possibilities? What do other people do? What materials could you use? Make a list of all your ideas—even the ones you don't think are good.

Step 3

Draw a plan.

Of all your ideas, choose the one you think is the best. Write it down. What do you need in order to make it work? Make a diagram to show all the parts and how each one works.

Step 4

Build a model.

Gather the materials you need. See if you can build parts of your idea that you can test one at a time. Ask for help.

You can get started on an invention of your own right away. Just follow the steps in "My Eight Steps of Inventing" to see how you can become a great inventor. Don't worry—you do not need to do it all by yourself.

Most inventions are not made by one person alone. Rather, teams of people work together to come up with answers. Ask someone you know to help you with your idea. When you team up to invent, you benefit from each other's knowledge and ideas. Besides, it can be fun!

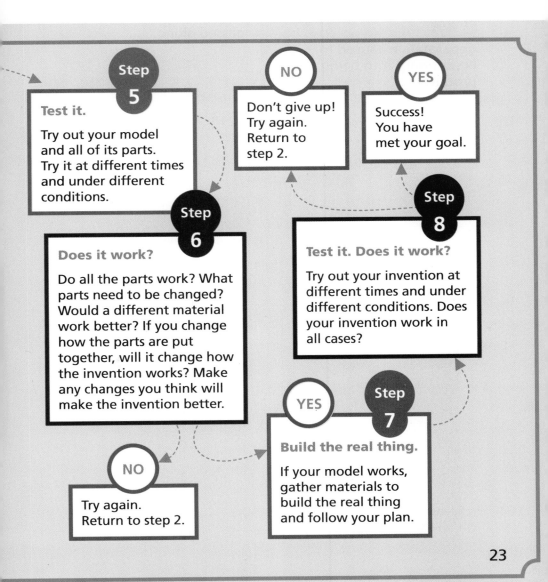

Step 5

Test it.

Try out your model and all of its parts. Try it at different times and under different conditions.

NO

Don't give up! Try again. Return to step 2.

YES

Success! You have met your goal.

Step 6

Does it work?

Do all the parts work? What parts need to be changed? Would a different material work better? If you change how the parts are put together, will it change how the invention works? Make any changes you think will make the invention better.

Step 8

Test it. Does it work?

Try out your invention at different times and under different conditions. Does your invention work in all cases?

NO

Try again. Return to step 2.

YES

Step 7

Build the real thing.

If your model works, gather materials to build the real thing and follow your plan.

23

Glossary

converts *v.* changes from one form to another.

devise *v.* to think out; plan or contrive; invent.

efficiency *n.* ability to produce the effect wanted without waste of time or energy.

generated *v.* caused to be; brought into being; produced.

percentage *n.* part of a whole number.

proclaimed *v.* made known publicly and officially.

reproduce *v.* to make a copy of.

transmitted *v.* sent along; passed along.